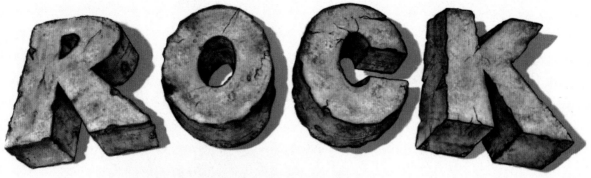

the boy who wanted to
ROCK

Written By David Weiser • Illustrated by Derek Lavoie

ISBN (hardcover): 978-0-578-79956-8
ISBN (paperback): 978-0-578-79957-5

Edited by Beth W. Patterson
Additional edits by Jef Rouner and Missy Upham
Book design by Rebecca LeGates, rebeccalegates.com

Orders, inquiries, and correspondence should be addressed to:
www.theboywhowantedtorock.com

Printed in the United States of America

For Arlen and Fennec

There once was a boy who wanted to rock
Sadly, this boy was in for a shock.

Things didn't go exactly the way
He thought they would when he first sat down to play.

The instruments all made a horrible noise!
This was quite different from playing with toys.

"This is too **hard!**" He stomped on the floor.

"**Ugh,** I give up!"
He stormed out the door.

He walked to the park,
he'd left in a huff.

He was starting to sulk,
when he heard a loud **"RUFF!"**

"**Hello,**" said a Dog, who seemed rather cheerful.
"Hi," the boy said, his face almost tearful.

"What have we here? What's got you down?"
"I want to play drums," the boy said with a frown.

"Tell me about it, let's walk for a while."
The way the dog wagged its tail made the boy smile.

"The sounds that I make are just barks, yips, and yelps,
But I know how to **count,** and I think that might help.

"Let's count to four as we step with our feet,
We'll make up a song, and you'll help keep the **beat.**"

Four beats bouncing all in a row
The beats give us **rhythm** and here's how they go:

3

Three's like one but not quite as strong
Just keep moving, you're coming along

CLAP

4

Four beats
starting over again
The beat gives us rhythm
and the rhythm never ends

BEACH

"Take what you've learned
and then notice what comes

When you practice your **counting**
while playing the drums."

Next, the boy wandered on down to the sea.
"And now the piano is bothering me."

An octopus heard and popped up to see him,
"Won't you come in for a musical swim?

"I don't have a keyboard," she said with a bubble,
"But learning some **notes** might help with your trouble.

"A musical **scale** is made up of eight,
Just watch my eight hands and I'll demonstrate.

"They're named after letters that you already know,
Repeat after me-here's how they go:

"C - D - E - F - G - A - B - C"

"After that they're the same, up high or down low,
You can play them quite fast, but it's best to start slow.

"Excellent work", the wise octopus said,
And gave the boy eight separate pats on the head.

"Take what you've learned and think of me please,
The next time you sit down to play on the **keys**."

He dried himself off and was feeling quite good,
"I'll just take this shortcut straight home through the woods...

One final challenge he needed to face:
"How to make sense of guitar and the bass?"

Just then he felt someone tousling his hair,
Two cats had appeared—as if out of thin air.

"I think I would start," one purred, strumming a chord,
"With strings," and the other cat's bass guitar roared!

"It's easy to get if we make up a song,
You'll be shredding and playing the lead before long!"

"Excellent work",
said the cats with a purr,
"With practice you'll get it,
of this we are sure!"

"So please think of us and
remember these things
The next time you rock out with frets
and with strings!"

The boy said goodbye to the cats with a wave
And ahead saw the great gaping mouth of a cave.

To go in or turn back—well, that was the choice,
Then up from the cave came a menacing voice:

"Who goes there?" it snarled, and it snorted "What's that?
"A boy who learns music from an octopus and cats?"

"And a dog!", yelled the boy, who was now quite afraid
That he might just get eaten—or worse—if he stayed!

"He'll need more than just counting and singing with fishes,
If becoming a **rocker** is what this boy wishes.

"Some parts of learning your rocks and your rolls...
Can only be taught by **goblins** and **trolls!**"

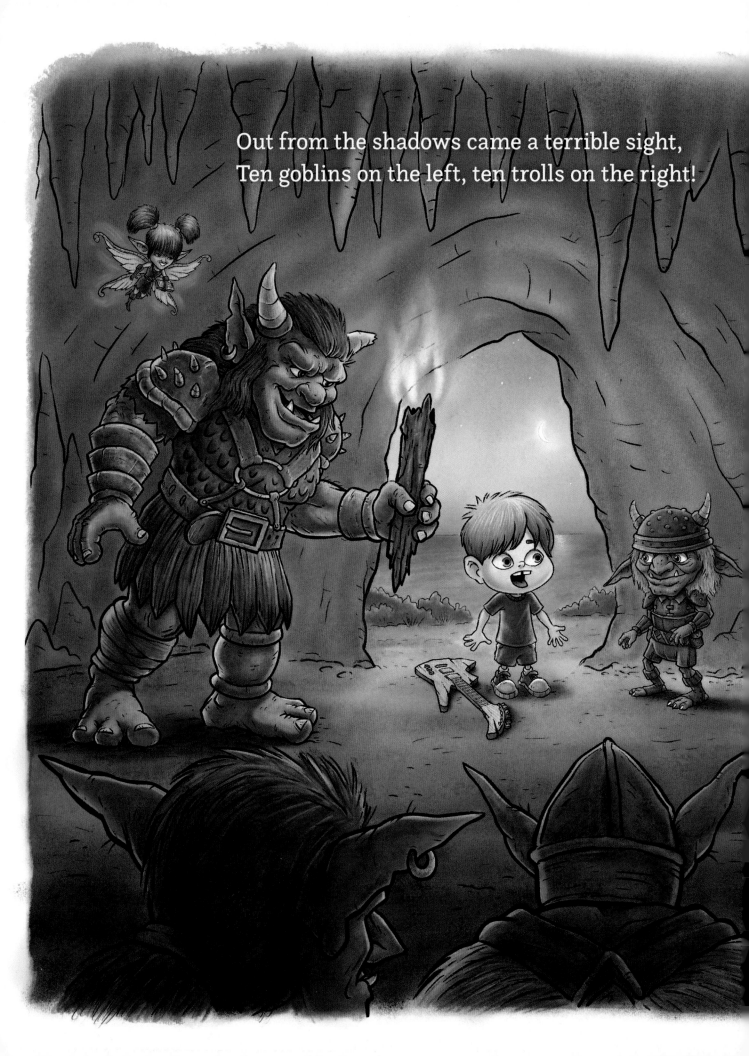

Out from the shadows came a terrible sight,
Ten goblins on the left, ten trolls on the right!

They hoisted him up,
this boy that they'd found,
And hauled him down tunnels
buried deep underground.

"If you want to rock properly,
you must learn how to **roar!**
You'll need fist-pumps and duck-walks
and hip-shakes and more!

"We'll teach you to **strut**
and to do it with swagger,
Just like we taught **Angus,**
Prince, and **Mick Jagger.**

"You'll choose your own look,
your own **style** and a theme,
When audiences see you,
they'll jump up and **scream!**

Fist Pump

Duck Walk

Hip Shake

"Now if it's not too much trouble, could you lend us a hand?
We could really use someone like **you** in our band."

They **rocked** and they rolled late into the night,
They practiced 'til each song was just about right.

And then in a flash, he was home in his bed,
Perhaps this **adventure** was all in his head?

He still had the cape, to his great disbelief!
No mullet, no Mohawk—whew! What a relief!

When he picked up his instruments the following day,
He tried to remember what his new friends would say:

Practice each day and you're sure to go far,
And the monster inside you will make you a star!

David Weiser has worked as a keyboard programmer with numerous Broadway, West End, touring, and televised musicals, including NBC's 2018 Jesus Christ Superstar, Phantom of the Opera, Cats, and Les Miserables. His credits also include work with high profile artists like David Bowie, The Who, and Brian Wilson. David lives outside of Boston with his wife, son, and a few goblins hanging about in the basement.

Derek Lavoie is a freelance illustrator and graphic designer whose work has appeared in a variety of places, from fine art magazines to the Team USA Olympic Luge race suit. He studied illustration at Mass College of Art in Boston, and now resides with his wife and son in upstate New York. When he's not drawing or painting, Derek can often be found tearing up local club gigs on bass guitar!

Thanks to our rockstar friends for all the inspiration!